MACHINES AT WORK

# A Backhoe's Day

by Betsy Rathburn
Illustrated by Mike Byrne

BELLWETHER MEDIA • MINNEAPOLIS, MN

**Blastoff! Missions** takes you on a learning adventure! Colorful illustrations and exciting narratives highlight cool facts about our world and beyond. Read the mission goals and follow the narrative to gain knowledge, build reading skills, and have fun!

Traditional Nonfiction

Narrative Nonfiction

Blastoff! Universe

## MISSION GOALS

> FIND YOUR SIGHT WORDS IN THE BOOK.

> LEARN ABOUT THE DIFFERENT PARTS OF A BACKHOE.

> FIND SOMETHING IN THE BOOK THAT YOU WOULD LIKE TO LEARN MORE ABOUT.

This edition first published in 2023 by Bellwether Media, Inc.

No part of this publication may be reproduced in whole or in part without written permission of the publisher. For information regarding permission, write to Bellwether Media, Inc., Attention: Permissions Department, 6012 Blue Circle Drive, Minnetonka, MN 55343.

Library of Congress Cataloging-in-Publication Data

LC record for A Backhoe's Day available at: https://lccn.loc.gov/2022013622

Text copyright © 2023 by Bellwether Media, Inc. BLASTOFF! MISSIONS and associated logos are trademarks and/or registered trademarks of Bellwether Media, Inc.

Editor: Christina Leaf    Designer: Andrea Schneider

Printed in the United States of America, North Mankato, MN.

This is **Blastoff Jimmy!** He is here to help you on your mission and share fun facts along the way!

# Table of Contents

| | |
|---|---|
| **Road Work** | 4 |
| **Pushing and Pulling** | 8 |
| **Many More Roads** | 20 |
| **Glossary** | 22 |
| **To Learn More** | 23 |
| **Beyond the Mission** | 24 |
| **Index** | 24 |

# Road Work

It is a quiet morning in the countryside. But it will be noisy soon.

The **construction site** is waking up. Workers begin to arrive. One climbs into the **cab** of a backhoe.

Inside the backhoe's **tractor**, the worker turns on the **engine**. It rumbles to a start.

Today, the backhoe has a big job. It is helping to build a road!

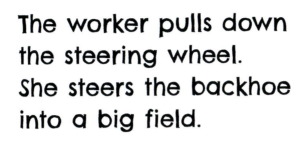

The worker pulls down the steering wheel. She steers the backhoe into a big field.

The backhoe's wide wheels easily move over the rough ground.

**JIMMY SAYS**

Backhoes are often used to move dirt and rocks. But they also move gravel, sand, and many other materials!

When the loader is full, the worker raises it. Time to dump!

The backhoe **levels** a row. When it reaches the end, it backs up. Beep, beep, beep!

The backhoe levels more rows. Now the land is flat for the new road!

leg

Next, the backhoe drives to the edge of the road.

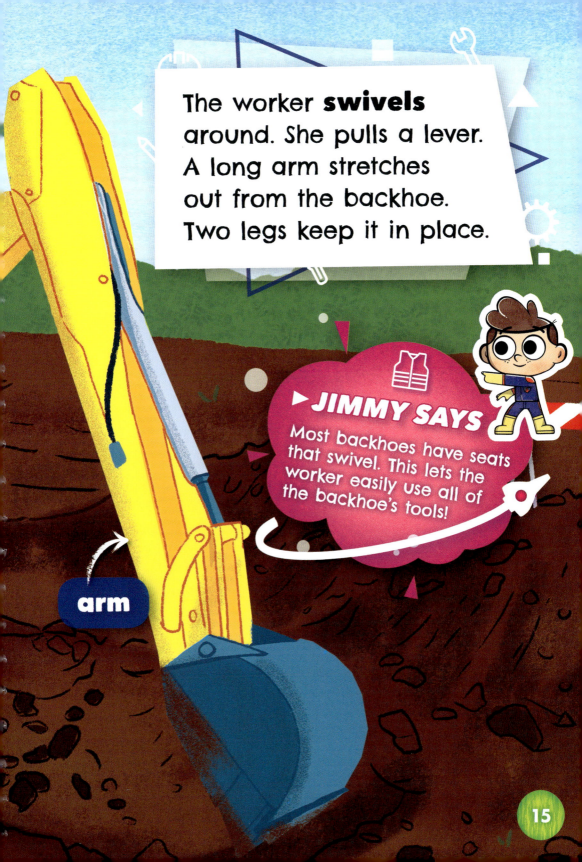

The arm's **bucket** digs into the ground. It pulls dirt and rocks toward the backhoe.

Then the bucket lifts to scoop up the dirt. It leaves behind a long, narrow **trench**.

bucket

▶ JIMMY SAYS ◀

Trenches are often built in and around roads. They hold pipes, cables, and other important items.

The worker dumps the dirt nearby. Then she turns back to the trench. It is not deep enough.

# Many More Roads

The backhoe's work here is finished. Tomorrow, more machines will come to finish the road. The backhoe has more work to do. It will travel all over the countryside!

# Glossary

**bucket**—the part of a backhoe that digs up dirt; the bucket is attached to a long arm.

**cab**—the place where the driver sits

**construction site**—a place where building projects are done

**engine**—the part of a backhoe that makes it go

**levels**—flattens

**loader**—the part of a backhoe that scrapes up dirt

**scrape**—to remove a layer of something by moving over it with something sharp

**swivels**—spins around

**tractor**—the part of a backhoe that holds the engine and the cab; the tractor is the main part of a backhoe.

**trench**—a long, narrow hole

# To Learn More

**AT THE LIBRARY**

Allan, John. *Let's Look at Diggers and Dumpers*. Minneapolis, Minn.: Hungry Tomato, 2019.

Kingston, Seth. *Backhoes*. New York, N.Y.: PowerKids Press, 2020.

Oxlade, Chris. *Construction Machines*. Buffalo, N.Y.: Firefly Books Ltd., 2018.

**ON THE WEB**

# FACTSURFER

Factsurfer.com gives you a safe, fun way to find more information.

1. Go to www.factsurfer.com.

2. Enter "backhoes" into the search box and click 🔍.

3. Select your book cover to see a list of related content.

# BEYOND THE MISSION

> WHAT IS ONE NEW FACT YOU LEARNED FROM THE BOOK?

> WHAT JOB WOULD YOU USE A BACKHOE FOR? WHY?

> DESIGN A NEW PART FOR A BACKHOE. WHAT DOES IT DO? WHAT JOBS DOES IT HELP WITH?

# Index

arm, 15, 16
bucket, 16, 19
cab, 4, 5
construction site, 4
countryside, 4, 20
dirt, 9, 10, 16, 18, 19
engine, 6
ground, 9, 16
job, 6, 21
legs, 14, 15
levels, 13
lever, 15
loader, 10, 11

materials, 9
road, 6, 13, 14, 20
rocks, 9, 10, 16
steering wheel, 9
swivels, 15
teeth, 10
tractor, 6, 7
trench, 16, 17, 18, 19
wheels, 8, 9
workers, 4, 6, 9, 10, 11, 15, 18

24